The story of Alma Mater parallels that of the city she loves to call her home.
Through reverses and disasters proportionately greater, she, too, has come
under the Providence of God, to the hour of manifest destiny. It becomes
your privilege and your sacred duty to help her onward to the heights...
Welcome to the University of San Francisco.

Father Hubert Flynn, S.J., Dean of the Faculties, 1931

From where I live, high on the hills of San Francisco, I look across a deep valley and other hills to one which tops them all and there, tall and gleaming in beauty, rise the spires of St. Ignatius. To you who may now know San Francisco, St. Ignatius is one of our oldest and most beautiful churches and college . But to us, who live near it daily, those two spires mean far more. Whatever your creed, they are a symbol of all that is best and bravest in city life. Before they were built, the hill on which they stand was merely sand dunes, littered with rubbish, ugly and forsaken. Then the city began to spread and the vision of men spread with it. And out of that vision came these lovely spires. In the adjacent school rooms many a civic leader has been trained. And only God knows how many shamed and bleeding hearts have found comfort before its soaring altar. When the great storms sweep out of the Pacific, darkening the town, or fog veils the valley in blue mist, I like to look towards those gleaming spires, which seem to float in another world.

Elsie Robinson's nationally syndicated column entitled, "Listen, World" as reprinted
in the USF Foghorn, December 16, 1949

THE UNIVERSITY OF

SAN FRANCISCO

Photographed by Phil Schermeister

HARMONY HOUSE

PUBLISHERS LOUISVILLE

Executive Editors: William Butler and William Strode
Library of Congress Catalog Number 86-083293
Hardcover International Standard Book Number 0-916509-24-9
Printed in USA by Pinaire Lithographing Corp., Louisville, Kentucky
First Edition printed Fall 1987 by Harmony House Publishers
P.O. Box 90, Prospect, Kentucky 40059 (502) 228-2010 / 228-4446

Photograph on page 37, "The Tradition Continues," is by Terry Heferdon.

Here let us build and wait; this will be the center of a great city.

Father Anthony Maraschi, S.J., ca. 1855

FOREWORD

One look at the University of San Francisco campus strikes a spark of wonder in each viewer's mind. What inspired such beauty? Certainly the city of San Francisco provides the stunning landscape, but what kind of people, what kind of experiences helped shape this campus and those that preceded it? This book may not answer these questions conclusively, but it will provide a memoir with heartwarming glimpses of the campus, its people and its character.

Those of us who have known the University for decades never tire of its vistas, of the rising sun casting light on the towers of St. Ignatius Church, the sunset as seen from the top of Lone Mountain or the drifting fog that changes these views.

I hope this book provides you with a vivid memory of USF's past, an understanding of the present and hopeful thoughts for the future. If you read between the lines and through the photographs, I am confident your impression will be a lasting one.

I also hope that as you look at these pages you will be inspired to return often to our hilltop campus.

John Lo Schiavo, S.J.
USF President

MEMORIES

Fr. Charles Dullea, S.J.
University Chancellor
President, 1963 to 1969

Over the fireplace in the student lounge of Campion Hall is engraved a verse from Vergil's Aeneid: "Forsan et haec olim meminisse juvabit"—Maybe some day you will enjoy remembering even these things.

Aeneas is talking to his band of Trojan warriors, refugees from the sack of Troy. "No strangers to affliction," they had passed between Scylla and Carybdis (ancient equivalent of the rock and the hard place), braved one-eye giant Cyclopes, and just now suffered a shipwreck of most of the fleet. They'd been cast up on the coast of Africa, discouraged and despondent. He cheers them up. "Maybe some day you will enjoy remembering even these things."

Remembering...what does the collective memory of the University of San Francisco go back to? Certainly a fair share of "even these things"—of often being between the rock and the hard place, facing the ogre of giant debt, of depressions, wars, earthquake and fire, total destruction. But there is always the resurrection. Not for nothing is the Phoenix, the mythical bird that rises from its own ashes, emblazoned on the University Center in the heart of the campus.

Let our collective memory wander back over the past 132 years, stimulated by glancing through the annals and archives, the yearbooks and the school papers, the gathered recollections of alumni and faculty and administrators.

Remembering...in no rigid order of time or category, but randomly, kaleidoscopically, in a free-flowing stream of consciousness...

Remembering...The beginning. Three buildings in the sand dunes on Market Street, between 4th and 5th, where the Emporium-Capwell building stands today. Frame buildings. The St. Ignatius Academy measured 16 by 26 feet. The "campus" 127 by 275 feet, less than an acre. Lot and buildings were financed by borrowed money, foreshadowing what was to come...The first day, October 15, 1855, three students showed up, greeted by three masters, a fine student-faculty ratio, for personal attention, the "cura personalis" of the Jesuit system.

This start was made in the middle of a major depression. When gold mining declined after the first boom of 1849-50, more than one-third of the city's 1,000 stores closed their doors. It took a special brand of courage to do what our Founders did. Better to call it faith.

Remembering...1862. New buildings constructed on the same site, as the school prospered. Great excitement on Market Street in 1876 as Fr. Joseph Neri, S.J., professor of physics, gave a demonstration of the new marvel of electricity for the thousands celebrating the first centennial of the Declaration of Independence. Other outstanding professors, Fr. Joseph Bayma, S.J., nationally and internationally known for his work in molecular physics, and Fr. Aloysius Varsi, S.J., scientist and mathematician trained in Paris...

1880. The move to Van Ness and Hayes streets. Imposing new buildings, on the site now occupied by Louise M. Davies Symphony Hall. Old timers said "old" St. Ignatius Church was even more impressive than the present one on Ignatian Heights.

1906. April 18. The great San Francisco earthquake and fire. Along with the city, the college, church, residence, classrooms, laboratories, library, theater, gymnasium, swimming pool—gone.

1906. September 1. New "temporary" buildings open on Hayes and Schrader streets. Diarist Father Henry Whittle, S.J., writes: "Our successors will not appreciate how difficult it was after so much had been destroyed in the city...to procure the various things in all departments"...The church and college destroyed, a new site acquired, new buildings erected—all in less than five months.

Remembering...When the debt was over a million dollars in 1919. Enter Father Richard Gleeson, S.J., and his friends and their heroic efforts to reduce it. The May Festival of 1921 that cleared $98,000...the "Biggest Whist Tournament in America," 4,800 players in the Civic Auditorium; another May Festival in 1924; getting the debt down to $150,000 by 1925.

Remembering...St. Ignatius College on the new site on Ignatian Heights...The former Masonic Cemetery acquired...St. Ignatius College becomes the University of San Francisco in 1930, the 75th anniversary...the "Grey Fog" becomes the "Dons"...A new era dawns.

Remembering...when USF played St. Mary's College in Kezar Stadium October 23, 1938. USF scored first and the San Francisco Chronicle ran a memorable photo of Danny Fisk, Bill Telesmanic and Dante Benedetti, in joyful exultation. The caption was "Joy that Died" because USF eventually lost the game. That was prophetic. All three players died in World War II.

Remembering...From the yearbooks, Al Braga's kick of 89 yards on the run against Montana...Johnny Swanson surprising the whole Loyola team by starting to return a punt and then himself punting on the run almost to the Loyola goal line...The "Cinderella Kids" in Madison Square Garden taking N.Y. by storm and winning the N.I.T....The Dons with Russell, Jones, and Co. winning 60 straight, and two NCAA championships in 1955 and 1956, and going to the final four in 1957...

The great football team of 1951, undefeated, untied and uninvited (to a bowl game because of black stars Ollie Matson and Burl Toler), the same team that graduated 9 players to the NFL, 4 of whom made All-Pro...Ollie Matson running in the Olympic Games in Helsinki with little time to train and still winning a medal. The great soccer teams under Gus Donoghue and Steve Negoesco: five NCAA championships.

Remembering...1964 and coeducation in all divisions. Women in the Green and Gold Room, in the clubs, in the rooting section. Women officers of the student body. Jo Ann Cahill first woman president of the Alumni Association. Mary Hile, first woman inducted into the Athletic Hall of Fame. Stephanie Woodhead, first woman A.S.U.S.F. president...

Remembering...The WWII years...The escape of President Manuel Quezon from Corregidor in the Philippines and the safe arrival of the presidential party in San Francisco. The solemn Te Deum in St. Ignatius Church in a thanksgiving service...Admiral Dan Callaghan, alumnus, commander of the cruiser "San Francisco" in the battle of the Java Sea. The monument at Land's End to him and the crew that perished...The big service flag hanging behind the altar in the church, a blue star for every alumnus in service and a gold star, 107 of them, for each one who had made the supreme sacrifice.

Remembering...the buildings going up and how proud we were at the developing campus: Gleeson Library in 1950, and Memorial Gym and Xavier Hall in the late 50's, after Phelan in 1955; then in the 60's, Kendrick, Harney, Gillson, Hayes-Healy, and the University Center, Cowell and the acquisition of the St. Ignatius High School property...George Gillson, dear little man, and his financing the landscaping of the campus, now no longer home of a "street car college"...

Remembering...the ceremonies, the special convocations, the solemn Masses in our great Italian Baroque church, with the choir and orchestra at full voice for the Baccalaureate Masses, the Mass of the Holy Spirit, for Easter and Christmas Midnight Mass...The great church bell. Made in England in 1859, it was the largest steel bell cast there until that time. It was acquired by the Fathers in 1862, and has been tolling its deep solemn tones in five successive St. Ignatius churches ever since.

Remembering...the faculty...Father Hubert (Hub) Flynn, S.J., dean, friend and teacher extraordinary, who knew Vergil's Aeneid by heart, and taught philosophy with wit and verve, quoting Immanuel Kant with a thick German accent...Fr. Peter Masten Dunne, S.J., with his

"take an A, old man" or "take an F, old man."...Doc Haley, Mr. Chips of the 30's and 40's who would take his botany classes on field trips to Golden Gate Park and come home alone, having somehow lost the class among the sylvan glades—and many, many, many more...

Remembering...The Special Events Committee: student initiative bringing to campus entertainers, philosophers, theologians and statesmen: Harry Belafonte, the Smothers Brothers, Gabriel Marcel, Karl Rahner, Henry Kissinger. Father Ray Feely, S.J., his lectures on Communism, and his required course on Marxism...Professor Ralph Lane's Students Western Addition Program, with over 100 SWAP members tutoring underprivileged kids...Dr. Giovanni Camajani's magnificent Schola Cantorum which delighted and enthused audiences in the Opera House and St. Ignatius Church...Fr. Andy Boss, S.J., and his Labor-Management School, training hundreds for industrial peace in the City...the versatile College Players, ranging in one season from Aeschylus's "Agamemnon" to Meredith Wilson's "Music Man"...The Philhistorians, founded in 1863, and still debating and orating...KUSF-FM, which grew to broadcast the voice of USF on Bay Area air waves.

Remembering our alumni...Two mayors of San Francisco, others

of other cities...one U.S. Senator...judges, a clutch of Pulitzer Prize winners and college presidents...innumerable public servants, business men and women, nurses and hospital administrators, university professors, scientists, doctors, lawyers, priests, sisters, brothers, teachers, principals, school superintendents, purveyors of all manner of good works..."Pro Urbe et Universitate," an education not only for the university, but also for the city, the country, the common good.

Remembering...1978 and the Lone Mountain acquisition after the Lone Mountain College ceased to exist...The option to buy, courtesy of the Religious of the Sacred Heart in return for USF's loan of $700,000 enabling the college to finish the academic year 1977-78...

A new dimension of spaciousness and beauty added to the campus...23 acres in the middle of a beautiful city, on top of a spectacular site commanding San Francisco Bay, the Golden Gate, the Pacific Ocean.

Handsome buildings, set in a wooded campus with quiet nooks and shady benches for study and meditation—a shelter from the busy city's bustle...A new measure of beauty added to what was once a street car campus.

Many memories, many traditions...As we turn the pages of this book we "will enjoy remembering these things."

Out around Park Avenue, where the Far West begins, we see, rising in triumph, the Twin Towers, companions in elegance and a Hilltop campus now clustered with buildings of distinction — some dedicated in the days of Father Edward Whelan, whose incessant labors made our wonder grow, some in the days of the gentle Gleeson, others in the era when Father Dunne's franchise as president was in fairest flower… May the hastening years make true the long-held dreams of those valiant ones whose works are worth the praises of this part of the earth — the early Jesuit Fathers now wreathed among the sainted dead, the dead who never die.

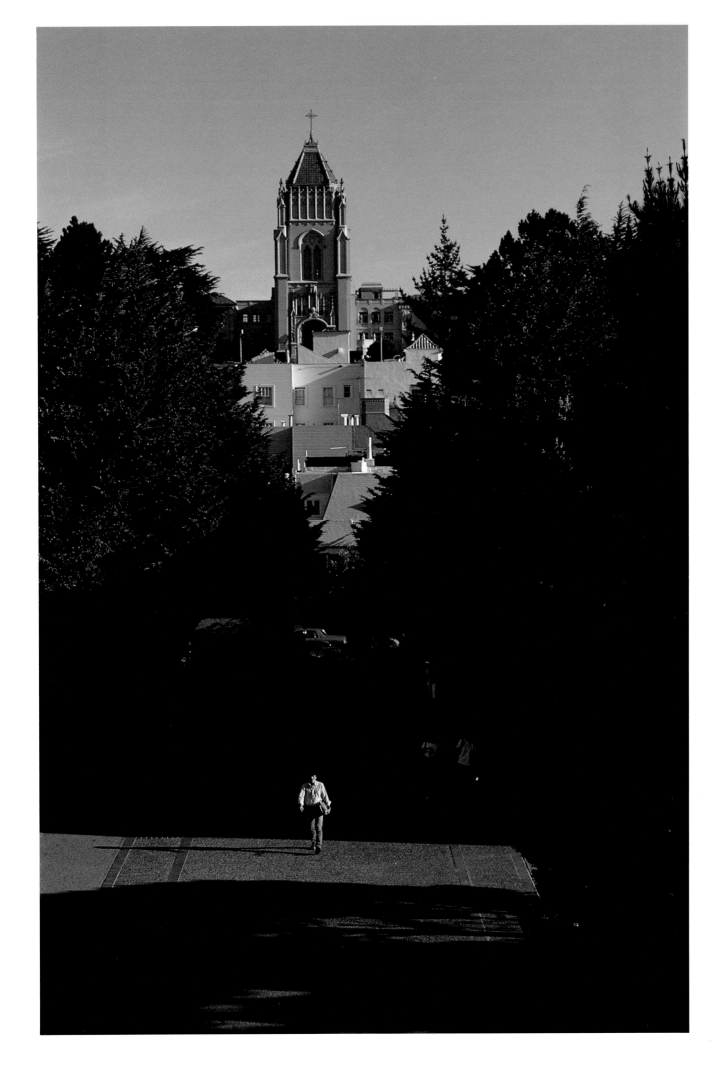

The university stands on these noble heights, its lights beaming as symbols to him who looks from home or hill, its lights within illuminating the minds and hearts of young men and women....

The Honorable Preston Devine, '25, San Francisco
Superior Court, 1959

Buildings adorn a campus and are necessary for the progress of the work; but we know that, ultimately, a university is as great as the truth taught within its walls, as those who teach that truth and those who, having received it, go forth to put it in practice as loyal children of God and citizens of America …

California Governor Goodwin J. Knight, 1956

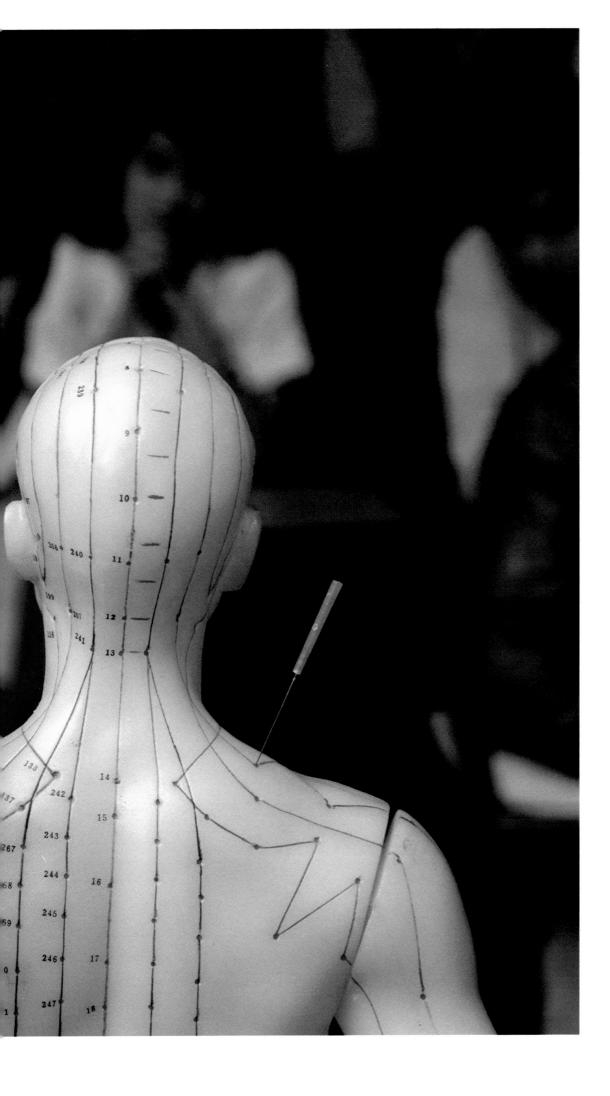

We tonight pay tribute to the founders of this University who built not only in wood, in brick, and in stone, but on the fleshy tablet of men's hearts; we hail them as great benefactors of church, city, state, and country and, mindful of the words of the prophet Isaiah: "Look unto the rock from which you were hewn"; we pledge them profound reverence and undying gratitude.

The Honorable Sylvester Andriano, Centennial Celebration, 1956

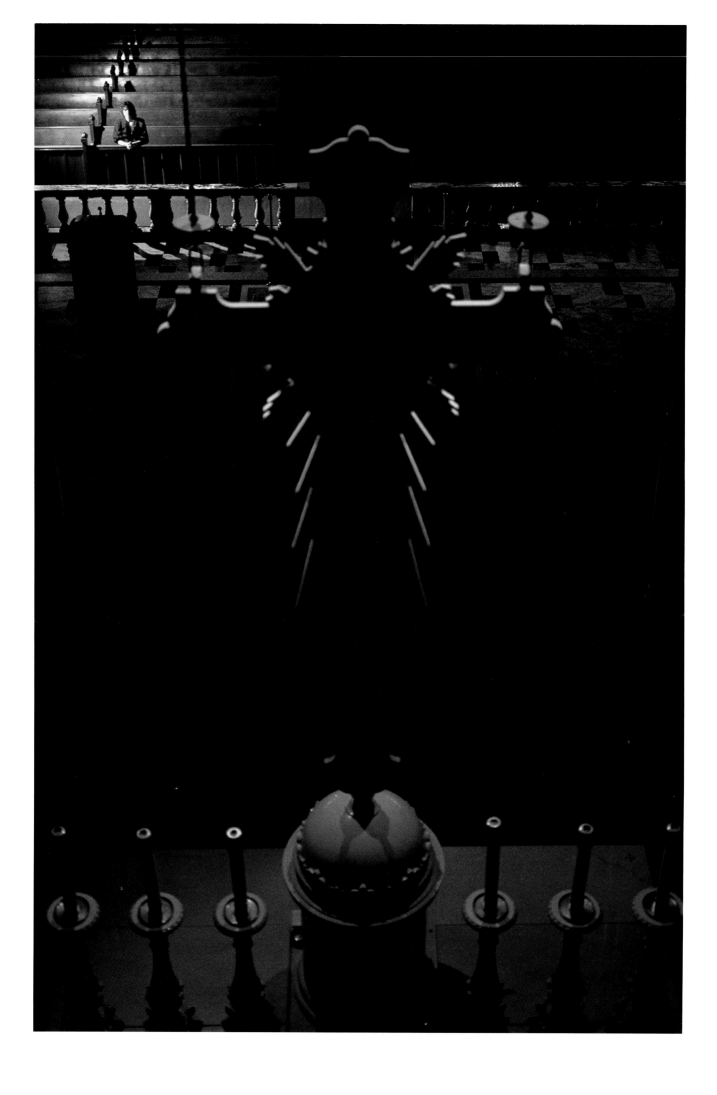

This Ignatian quality explains only half of what constitutes this university.
This school is not only Jesuit in character, it is also supremely "San Franciscan."
In a striking fashion, it has both served the bay area since 1855, and its own
history has closely paralleled that of this "cool, great peninsula of love."

Monsignor James P. Gaffey, '62, at 125th anniversary commemorative
mass, October 11, 1980

The "great bell" of St. Ignatius Church

Harney Plaza

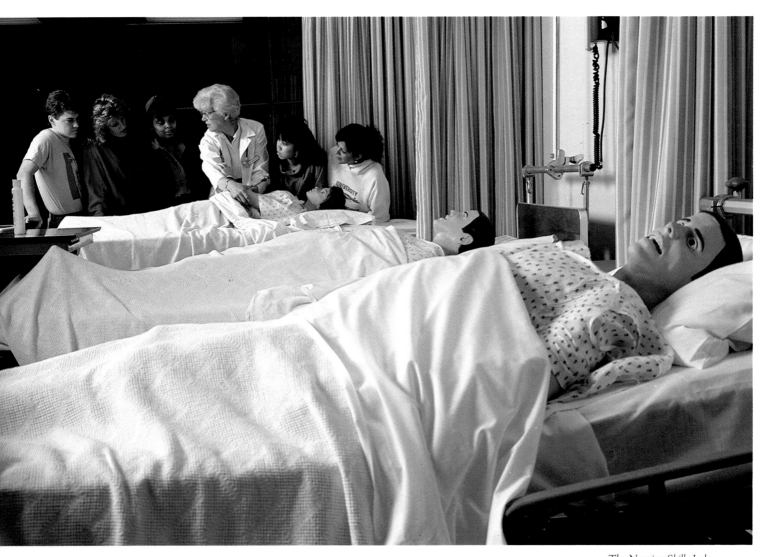

The Nursing Skills Lab

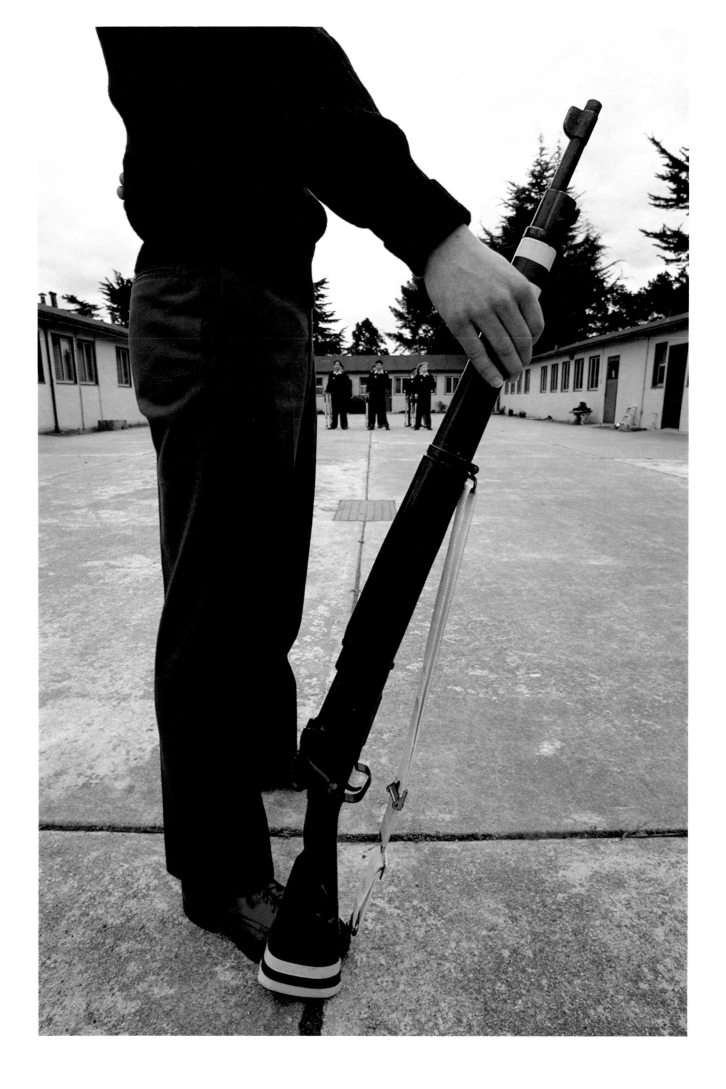

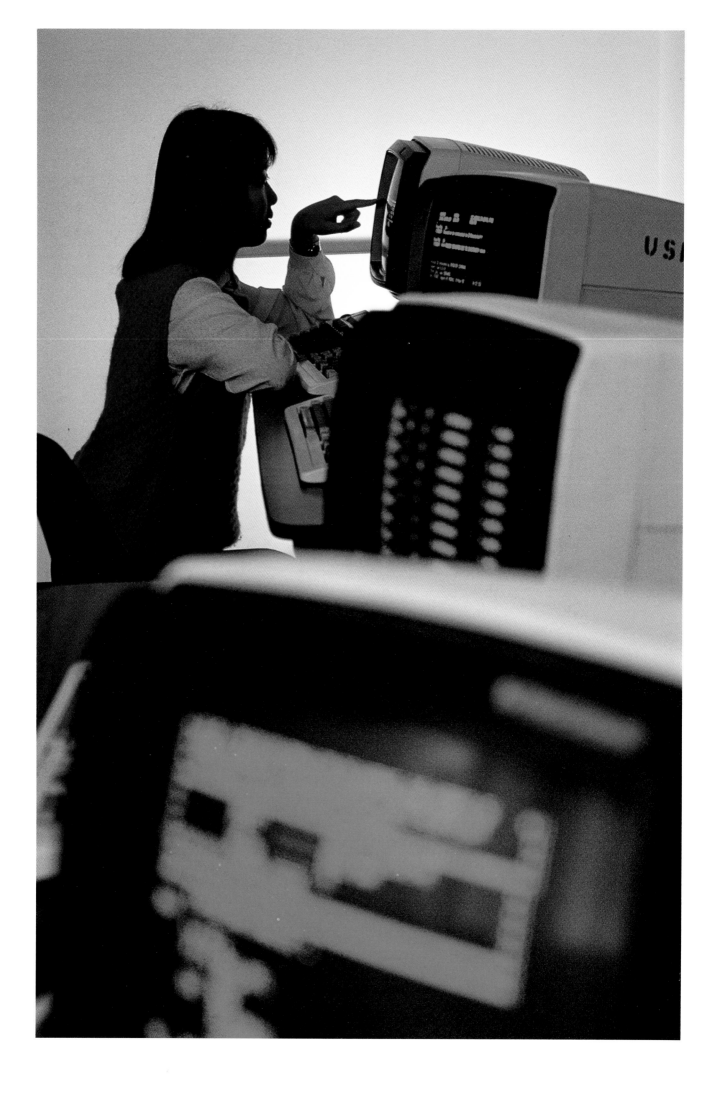

Time and ivy will mellow its beautiful lines. But built into its very fabric are many things – the tradition of 50 years of public service by graduates of the school…. a half century of devoted and scholarly instruction, that has raised the teaching of law from a vocational training to the plane of a social science.

The Honorable Herman Phleger, at dedication of Kendrick Hall, 1962

The building of this structure will be an aid to bring back to men the idea that, without faith and without belief, there can be no salvation come to men. The towers of this structure will point ever towards God…this, then, is to be a new fortress for Christ here in San Francisco.

The Rev. Joseph Gleason, March 1912, at the cornerstone-laying of St. Ignatius Church.

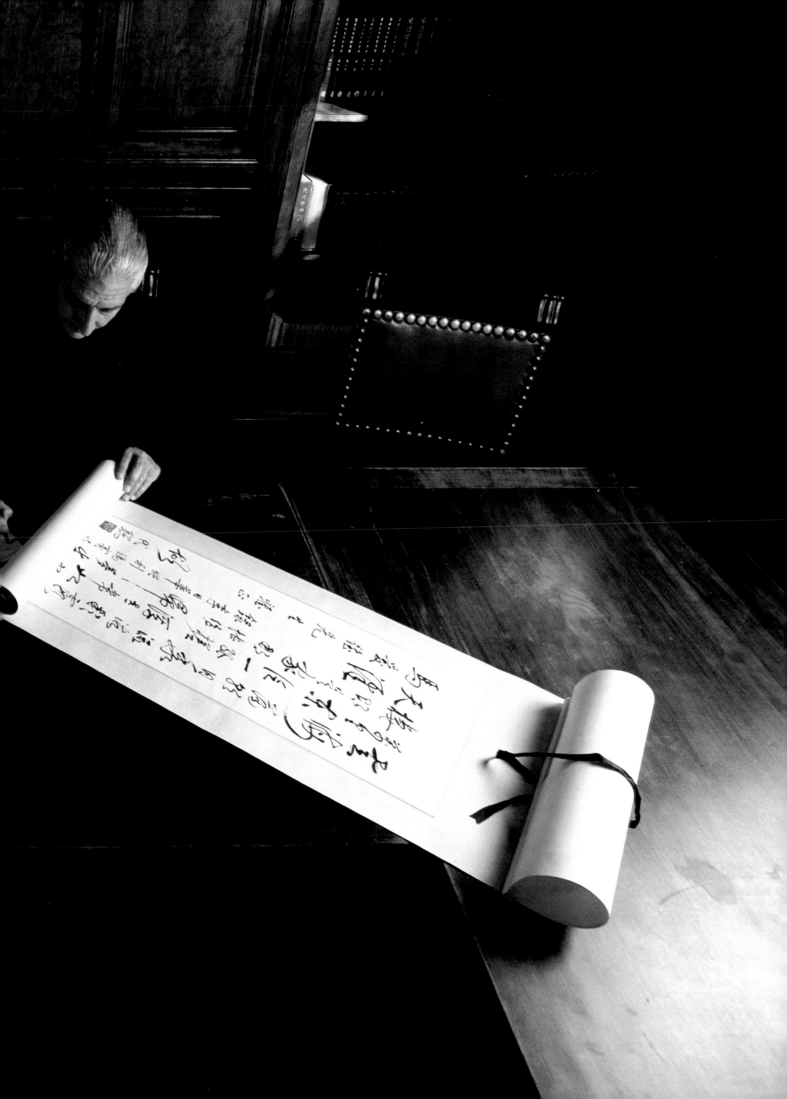

In the moments of solemnity and serenity which follow conferring of degrees, in the hearts of those leaving the University, there wells up a love for the institution which now, truly, is their Alma Mater.

The Honorable Preston Devine,'25, June 11, 1955

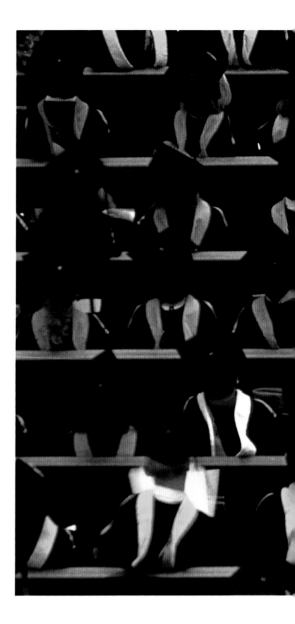

...your University stands for one hundred years of progress. A progress that has seen great men in all walks of life emerge from her classrooms. Great men that have made their mark upon the world and laid their trophies at her feet. It is to you that the burden falls to carry on a glorious tradition. Your task in the future is to insure the eminence of Alma Mater. Take up the Green and Gold and carry it well for all to see! You have an obligation to USF and its founding fathers to further its ideals.

San Francisco Foghorn, Centennial edition, 1955

THE UNIVERSITY
AND THE PAST

GLIMPSES OF THE UNIVERSITY
OF SAN FRANCISCO IN IMAGES
FROM THE ARCHIVES

San Francisco in 1856. The area shown is the approximate site of USF today.

Father Anthony Maraschi, S.J., the founder of the University of San Francisco.

This drawing is of the first site of St. Ignatius Church and College in 1855. The structures stood on sand dunes on Market Street, between 4th and 5th, where the Emporium-Capwell Building stands today.

In 1862 this handsome brick structure replaced the wooden originals, and remained until 1880, when the College moved to a new location.

The Chemistry Lab of St. Ignatius College looked like this in 1890.

The College moved to these larger, more impressive structures at Van Ness and Hayes Streets in 1880. Governor George Perkins at its dedication remarked, "The edifice you have raised must redound to the advantage of Christianity, and future years will consecrate the devotion you have so unfalteringly and unsparingly bestowed on this great work dedicated to science, learning and morality."

Another view of the College at Hayes and Van Ness, approximately 25 years later, circa 1905.

To those who do not desire a classical education, the ordinary commercial branches will be taught. Any young man who may desire to acquire knowledge in the fullest sense has here an opportunity which few in this country possess. San Francisco is, we believe, the only city in the United States which is so blessed.

The Bulletin,1893

St. Ignatius Gymnasium, 1906

The Sanctuary, St. Ignatius Church, circa 1906. According to Fr. Charles Dullea, S.J., old-timers say this 'old' St. Ignatius "was even more impressive than the present one on Ignatian Heights."

Great San Francisco Fire

After the earthquake and fires in April, 1906, the College stood in ruins.

Temporary buildings at Hayes and Shrader Streets (nicknamed "The Shirt Factory") became the 4th site of St. Ignatius Church and College.

left, San Francisco burned following the earthquake on April 18, 1906. The College burned from an accidental king fire that spread through the block of Van Ness Avenue.

September 7, 1906 — The first day of class at St. Ignatius College's "Shirt Factory" campus. Students assembled amid the construction of new buildings.

...arly a quarter of a century later, in 1929, St. Ignatius finished its last session at "The Shirt Factory," as a new facility was built ...Ignatian Heights, the College's 5th site. Heroic fund-raising efforts by Fr. Richard Gleeson, S.J., had begun in 1919. On its ...th Anniversary in 1930, St Ignatius College officially became the University of San Francisco.

The Sanctuary of the new St. Ignatius Church, 1930.

Exterior of the "new" St. Ignatius Church in 1930.

USF campus, circa 1932.

San Francisco's unforgettable NCAA Championship basketball team of 1955-56 was anchored by two legends, K.C. Jones...

...and Bill Russell, both of whom went on to further glory with the Boston Celtics.